YOUR KNOWLEDGE HAS VALUE

- We will publish your bachelor's and master's thesis, essays and papers

- Your own eBook and book - sold worldwide in all relevant shops

- Earn money with each sale

Upload your text at www.GRIN.com
and publish for free

Youth and Sexuality. The Vital Role of Sexuality in Young People's Development

Kimberley Bartolo

Bibliographic information published by the German National Library:

The German National Library lists this publication in the National Bibliography; detailed bibliographic data are available on the Internet at http://dnb.dnb.de.

ISBN: 9783346438478
This book is also available as an ebook.

Print and binding: Books on Demand GmbH, Norderstedt, Germany
Printed on acid-free paper from responsible sources.

The present work has been carefully prepared. Nevertheless, authors and publishers do not incur liability for the correctness of information, notes, links and advice as well as any printing errors.

GRIN web shop: https://www.grin.com/document/1031645

Youth and Sexuality

Sexuality Plays a Vital Role in Young People's Development. Discuss.

Kimberley Bartolo

B.A. (Hons) in Social Wellbeing Studies

Table of Contents

Introduction

Young people are sexual beings and so just as it is crucial to strengthen one's cognitive, physical and emotional growth, it is also crucial to instigate sexual growth (Huberman, 2016). Sexuality evolves from a person's interactions with him/herself and from relationships with others (Symons, 1979). Development of sexuality is an ongoing process which starts at conception and continues to develop throughout the person's lifespan (Kar, Choudhury & Singh, 2015). Young people start sexually developing into adults and along the way they face a lot of physical; biological; and social changes. That is why most of the time this stage is referred to as being a critical stage in a young person's development process (Wood et al., 2017).

Pubertal Changes in Youths' Sexual Development

One of the most significant rapid and dramatic changes in a young person's sexual development happen during the stages of puberty (Marcia, 1980; Alsaker, 1995). During this time, young people start experiencing physical and biological changes within their bodies. For instance, girls' breasts will start to grow; hips may widen; pubic hair will start to develop; and their menstrual cycles may start. On the other hand, boys experience their genitals starting to grow; facial hair will start to develop; and their larynx gets larger (Attwood, 2008; McBride, 2010). Both genders experience getting taller in height and gaining some weight (Hayward, 2003). Additionally, both genders will have the capability of reproducing (Johnson & Barber, 2009). Males and females experience puberty at different ages, with females often starting earlier than males. A females' pubertal cycle tends to be shorter than a males' cycle (McBride, 2010; Kar, Choudhury & Singh, 2015).

All of these bodily changes challenge the sexual identity of the young person. Considering that young people are going through a lot of physical; biological; and psychological changes, they might feel stressed since they are unable to cope with all of these changes happening all at once (Kar, Choudhury & Singh, 2015; Villanueva, 2015), and might feel as if they no longer knows who they are. Young people going through puberty tend to become more concerned with their appearances (Pickhardt, 2016). Some young people might feel unhappy with their bodies and the way that they look. There are certain cultures which impose the idea of needing to have a particular type of body, like for example American girls being slim and boys being muscular (Thies & Travers, 2005). This can increase the stress levels in young people even more during this crucial period in their life and may result in being unhappy with their body image, since they start to compare themselves a lot with these ideal type of bodies (Pickhardt, 2016). Young people that develop earlier than others, like for instance a female starts to have her breasts grow before her peers and so she needs to start wearing a bra before them which might make her feel awkward, or later than others, like for instance a male has not yet started to shave his bear but all of his peers have, tend to be the ones most unhappy with the way they look (Thies & Travers, 2005; Pickhardt, 2016). This is because they might feel embarrassed and shy that their peers are not experiencing the same things as them and vice-versa (Brennan, 2014). In general, young males tend to view their biological changes as being something positive, while young females tend to look at it as being something negative (Martin, 1996; Pickhardt, 2010). These different feelings towards puberty, from both genders, come from the old taboos and stigmas that occurred in the past. There used to be this believe that every action, sexually oriented, made by a woman was made to tempt a man for example, from the clothes they wear and the photos they took (Hudson, 2016). Young females feel shame towards their own bodies. This is because it was seen that by expressing their sexuality, they were being 'sluts' while, males were seen to be 'cool' and 'macho' (Martin, 1996; Smith, Moore & Rosenthal, 2016).

However, this is not always the case. Not all young people react to puberty in the same way. For some it is an exciting process rather than an embarrassing and challenging one (Ashford & LeCroy, 2010; Lewis, 2016). Some young people might have a smoother transition than others. Indeed, Martin (1996) interviewed several young people and some of them stated how puberty, hence their sexual development, was 'no big deal'. For example, one of the young females interviewed said that starting her period did not make her feel unhappy towards her own body, but she was rather happy. This was also seen in the interviews done by Fingerson (2006), where one of the young females that was interviewed spoke about how having her menstruation is not something shameful and embarrassing, but how she looks at it as being normal and not a big deal. Furthermore, research shows that when young people are prepared for puberty, hence they are well informed about the changes that occur throughout this process, they handle it better (Lewis, 2016). So for instance, when a young male is well informed about his first ejaculation, when it occurs, he would have been prepared for it and so he knows it is normal (Attwood, 2008; Greenberg, Bruess, & Conklin, 2011).

Interactions: Intra and Inter Personal

There are various ways by which young people can interact sexually. Young persons start experiencing sexual behaviours whilst they are going through the stages of development (Araji, 2004). Such behaviours change and start to occur throughout their interactions. There are mainly two forms of interactions; intrapersonal and interpersonal.

Intrapersonal. This occurs between one's self and it is about understanding one's own likes and dislikes (Curran, 2015). This form of interaction includes in random and exploratory behaviours by the young person, which mainly involves the self. Usually, such behaviours are instigated by exploration and curiosity (Araji, 2004). Intrapersonal behaviours include in masturbation and sexual fantasizing (Chi, Van de Bongardt & Hawk, 2014). Additionally, some young persons may also start inserting fingers or objects into their body openings so that they explore what is pleasurable and what hurts them (Araji, 2004). Research indicates that young males engage in this behaviour more frequently than young females (Chi, Van de Bongardt & Hawk, 2014).

Interpersonal. This involves having interactions with other people rather than between one's self (Curran, 2015). In this form of interaction, young people develop sexual attractions towards other persons and as a result they might start dating and some even engage in sexual relationships. Such interpersonal behaviours may involve in young males comparing penis size and young females showing off their breasts to each other; oral sex; and sexual intercourse. Usually, such behaviours are either driven by intention or happen spontaneously (Araji, 2004). However, not all young people feel ready to involve themselves sexually with others. Some might delay interacting sexually with other people for various reasons, such as waiting for the 'right' person or waiting till a particular age. By contrast, others are simply happy with the fact that they can say 'no' (Heywood, Patrick, Pitts, & Mitchell, 2015; Williams, 2016). Furthermore, other young people might choose not to engage in sexual relationships due to their culture, for example if the young person was raised in a home were sex was seen as something 'dirty' or was a topic which was not spoken about, then the person might view sexual activity in that manner as well (Araji, 2004). Lastly, other reasons why young people might choose to involve or not involve themselves sexually with others are peer influence and social context. A lot of young people, especially boys, feel pressured by their peers to engage in sexual relationships before they themselves feel ready to (Allen, 2003; Carroll, 2012). If, the young person goes out a lot, especially to discos and so on, then one is more tempted to engage sexually with others for instance, due to alcohol (Jackson, Sher, & Park, 2006).

The decision about whether or not, one should engage or not engage in sexual relationships requires a lot of thinking and it is not something that should happen 'just to get it over with'. Yet, in some cases, this is the reason behind why young people decide to engage in sexual relationships (Machin & Leeuwen, 2007; Rufus, 2009). Tough overall, the majority of young people are happy with whatever decision they made (Williams, 2016).

Sexuality Education

The term 'sexuality' remains one that holds a lot of connotations with it. Its definition varies from one person to another, depending on what the person believes it is and the context it is used in. Nonetheless, a common understanding of the word is that it varies from the term sex; although they are very much related. Sexuality is about who you are rather than what you do. There is still a lot disagreement between educators about what exactly should be included in sexuality education (Schroeder, 2009; Bruess & Schroeder, 2014). However, an agreement amongst some of the topics that should be learned are sexual health; relationships; sexual intimacy; and human sexuality (Ponzetti, 2016).

As mentioned earlier, one way how stress, awkwardness and embarrassment of sexual development and puberty can be eased is through education. When young people are prepared and properly informed about this process they are able to handle it better (Attwood, 2008; Greenberg, Bruess, & Conklin, 2011; Lewis, 2016). It will also help them understand what to expect and what certain things mean, such as sexual arousal.

Moreover, sexuality education is not only important for that reason. Educating young people about sexuality and how to handle it benefits them as well. Being more educated about the topic, they can understand more the dangers and consequences that it can have on them, like for example unplanned pregnancies and diseases (Smith et al., 2016; Williams, 2016). So, whilst young people need to explore their sexuality through sexual activity, they still need to have the necessary information and knowledge, so that they develop safe and enjoyable sexual behaviour (Smith et al., 2016; FPA, 2017). In fact, research indicates that when young people, in particular young females, are well informed about relationships and sex, their chances of reporting poor sexual health outcomes is lower, when compared to those who lack information (Ministry for health, 2011; FPA, 2018). Yet, sexuality education should not only be oriented towards teaching young people preventative measures to avoid the negative consequences related to sexuality but, should also teach respect for both one's self and others. It should also be about embracing sexual feelings as being gifts, which means that they should be cherished (Schroeder, 2009). Sometimes, the media portrays sexuality as being something that in reality it is not. Some young people have false perceptions about what they should expect from their sexual relationships and how it should be (Gruber & Grube, 2000). Consequently, at times, some young people end up feeling disappointed with their sexual experiences since, they compare it to what they have seen on the media.

Alcohol consumption also plays a role in a young person's sexuality development. This is because during this process, young people are at a stage were they are going out more hence, their alcohol consumption is higher. Research indicates that alcohol consumption lowers people's inhibitions (Johnson & Barber, 2009; Jackson et al., 2016). This means that they are more likely to do things that they would not normally do like for example, some young people end up engaging with others sexually. More often than not, this causes unplanned and unprotected sex which can then lead to unwanted pregnancies and diseases, such as AIDS or sexually transmitted diseases (STD) (Moore, Rosenthal, & Mitchell, 1996; Araji, 2004; Heywood et al., 2015). If, young people were more educated and knowledgeable about such negative outcomes, then they could avoid having such risky sex behaviours (Smith et al., 2016). Additionally, some young people end up having sex with their partners to avoid disappointing them, as they fear that if they say no, their relationship will end (Alman, 2018; Russell, 2018). It is important that young people understand that saying 'no' is okay, especially if, they feel that they are not ready to engage in sexual behaviour with others just yet. This can all be learned through sexuality education (Schroeder, 2009).

Conclusion

Sexuality plays a major role in a young person's development and understanding such a process is of outmost importance (Kar et al., 2015). It is a process that brings a lot of changes within the young person's life (Wood et al., 2017), especially when the young person hits the pubertal stage (Marcia, 1980; Alsaker, 1995). As discussed above, young people react differently to puberty; some have positive attitudes towards it, while others have negative ones. Young people tend to explore their sexuality through different interactions, either with others or their selves, as they are still learning about their; likes, dislikes, feelings and relationships (Araji, 2004). In conclusion, a way to ease some of this stressful developmental process that young people go through is by properly informing them about it.

That way, they can be prepared for what to expect (Attwood, 2008). For this reason, sexuality education should be practised more both within schools by educators and at home by the parents.

References

Allen, C. (2003, May 1). Peer pressure and teen sex: many teens, especially boys, feel pressure to have sex before they are ready. According to recent research, some 63 percent of teens believe that waiting to have sex is a good idea, but few people actually do. *Psychology Today*. Retrieved January 13, 2019 from https://www.psychologytoday.com/intl/articles/200305/peer-pressure-and-teen-sex

Alman, I. (2018, February 4). When your partner says no to sex: being refused need not be the end of the word, just a disappointment. *Psychology Today*. Retrieved January 13, 2019 from https://www.psychologytoday.com/us/blog/sex-sociability/201802/when-your-partner-says-no-sex

Alsaker, F. D. (1995). Timing of puberty and reactions to pubertal changes. In Rutter, M. (Eds.), *Psychosocial disturbances in young people: Challenges for prevention*, pp. 37-82. Cambridge, U. K.: The press syndicate of the University of Cambridge (Cambridge University Press).

Araji, S. K. (2004). Preadolescents and adolescents: Evaluating normative and non-normative sexual behaviours and development. In Reilly, G. O., Marshall, W. L., Carr, A., & Beckett, R. (Eds.), *The handbook of clinical intervention with young people who sexually abuse*, pp. 3-35. Retrieved https://books.google.com.mt/books?id=7L15AgAAQBAJ&pg=PA10&dq=young+people+sexual+interactions&hl=en&sa=X&ved=0ahUKEwicrZOPhObfAhWGCSwKHWM3CP8Q6AEILTAB#v=onepage&q=young%20people%20sexual%20interactions&f=false

Ashford, J. B., & LeCroy, C. W. (2010). *Human behaviour in the social environment: A multidimensional perspective* (4th Ed.). Retrieved from https://books.google.com.mt/books?id=R8-HitN5Jp0C&pg=PA420&dq=young+people+prepared+for+puberty&hl=en&sa=X&ved=0ahUKEwi8v5ip_eXfAhWFjiwKHYGyBMcQ6AEILDAB#v=onepage&q=young%20people%20prepared%20for%20puberty&f=false

Attwood, S. (2008). *Making sense of puberty: A forthright guide to puberty, sex and relationships for people with Asperger's syndrome*. Retrieved from https://books.google.com.mt/books?id=xLqwYAzogiwC&printsec=frontcover&dq=sexuality+and+puberty&hl=en&sa=X&ved=0ahUKEwjCz-

Xi7eXfAhVGDSwKHdKeDpAQ6AEIOjAD#v=onepage&q=sexuality%20and%20pu
berty&f=false

Brennan, N. (2014, October 31). I was a late developer. *The Guardian.* Retrieved January 11,
2019 from https://www.theguardian.com/lifeandstyle/2014/oct/31/i-was-a-late-
developer

Bruess, C. E., & Schroeder. (2014). *Sexuality Education: Theory and practice* (6th Ed.).
Retrieved from https://books.google.com.mt/books?id=WWFW6-
kkAVoC&pg=PA203&dq=sexuality+education&hl=en&sa=X&ved=0ahUKEwjA_M
OmhejfAhUviKYKHaALBI0Q6AEIMTAC#v=onepage&q=sexuality%20education&
f=false

Carroll, J. L. (2012). *Discovery series: Introduction to Human sexuality.* Retrieved from
https://books.google.com.mt/books?id=naoJAAAAQBAJ&pg=RA1-
PA198&dq=peer+influence+and+sexual+relationships&hl=en&sa=X&ved=0ahUKE
wjg9p3xt-
bfAhXkposKHW1eDp0Q6AEIRTAG#v=onepage&q=peer%20influence%20and%20
sexual%20relationships&f=false

Chi, X., Van de Bongardt, D., & Hawk, S. (2014). Intrapersonal and interpersonal sexual
behaviours of Chinese university students: Gender differences in prevalence and
correlates. *The Journal of Sex Research, 52*(5), pp. 532-542. Retrieved from
https://www.researchgate.net/publication/261596080_Intrapersonal_and_Interpersona
l_Sexual_Behaviors_of_Chinese_University_Students_Gender_Differences_in_Preva
lence_and_Correlates

Curran, L. (2015, June 28). *Intrapersonal and interpersonal relationships* [Video file].
Retrieved on January 12, 2019 from https://www.youtube.com/watch?v=q-
Su2ecYJnc

Fingerson, L. (2006). *Girls in power: Gender, body, and menstruation in adolescence.* New
York, N.Y.: State University of New York Press.

FPA (the sexual health charity). (2017). Young people and sexuality policy [PDF file].
Retrieved from https://www.fpa.org.uk/sites/default/files/young-people-policy-
statement.pdf

FPA (the sexual health charity). (2018). Relationships and sex education (RSE) policy [PDF
file]. Retrieved from https://www.fpa.org.uk/sites/default/files/relationships-and-sex-
education-policy-statement.pdf

Greenberg, J. S., Bruess, C. E., & Conklin, S. C. (2011). *Exploring the dimensions of human sexuality* (4th Ed.). Retrieved from https://books.google.com.mt/books?id=1NC5R0RozBYC&pg=PA397&dq=young+pe ople+prepared+for+puberty&hl=en&sa=X&ved=0ahUKEwi8v5ip_eXfAhWFjiwKH YGyBMcQ6AEIMzAC#v=onepage&q=young%20people%20prepared%20for%20pu berty&f=false

Gruber, E., & Grube, J. W. (2000). Adolescent sexuality and the media: a review of current knowledge and implications. *The Western Journal of Medicine, 172*(3), pp. 210-214. Retrieved from https://www.ncbi.nlm.nih.gov/pmc/articles/PMC1070813/

Hayward, C. (Ed.). (2003). *Gender differences at puberty.* Cambridge, U.K.: The press syndicate of the University of Cambridge (Cambridge University Press).

Heywood, W., Patrick, K., Pitts, M., & Mitchell, A. (2015). "Dude, I'm seventeen… It's okay not to have sex by this age": Feelings, reasons, pressures, and intentions reported y adolescents who have not had sexual intercourse. *The Journal of Sex Research, 53*(9), pp. 1-8. Retrieved from https://www.researchgate.net/publication/287796845_Dude_I'm_Seventeen_It's_Oka y_Not_to_Have_Sex_by_This_Age_Feelings_Reasons_Pressures_and_Intentions_Re ported_by_Adolescents_Who_Have_Not_Had_Sexual_Intercourse

Huberman, B. (2016). Growth and development, ages 13 to 17-what parents need to know. *Advocates for youth.* Retrieved December 31, 2018 from https://advocatesforyouth.org/resources/health-information/parents-16/

Hudson, V. (2016, May 17). Being a sexual being is not just about having sex. *Her campus at Arizona.* Retrieved January 11, 2019 from https://www.hercampus.com/school/arizona/being-sexual-being-not-just-about-having-sex

Jackson, K. M., Sher, K. J., & Park, A. (2006). Drinking among college students: consumption and consequences. In Galanter, M. (Ed.), *Recent developments in alcoholism. Alcohol problems in adolescents and young adults: Epidemiology, neurobiology, prevention and treatment,* pp. 84-93. New York, N.Y.: Kluwer Academic/Plenum Publishers.

Johnson, E. L. & Barber, D. E. (2009). *A smoother transition: Why teenagers make rational and irrational choices.* Retrieved from https://books.google.com.mt/books?id=ygGttVZnMtcC&pg=PA6&dq=smooth+transi tion+into+puberty&hl=en&sa=X&ved=0ahUKEwjAv9mfu-

XfAhVK1iwKHedeAOoQ6AEIJzAA#v=onepage&q=smooth%20transition%20into
%20puberty&f=false

Kar, S. K., Choudhury, A., & Singh, A. P. (2015). Understanding normal development of
adolescent sexuality: a bumpy ride. *Journal of human reproductive sciences, 8*(2), 70-
74. Retrieved from https://www.ncbi.nlm.nih.gov/pmc/articles/PMC4477452/

Lewis, V. (2016). *No body's perfect: A helper's guide to promoting positive body image in
children and young people.* Retrieved from
https://books.google.com.mt/books?id=9BZ0DwAAQBAJ&pg=PA74&dq=young+pe
ople+prepared+for+puberty&hl=en&sa=X&ved=0ahUKEwi8v5ip_eXfAhWFjiwKH
YGyBMcQ6AEIJzAA#v=onepage&q=young%20people%20prepared%20for%20pub
erty&f=false

Machin, D., & Leeuwen, T. V. (2007). *Global media discourse: A critical introduction.*
Abingdon, Oxon: Routledge.

Marcia, J. E. (1980). Identity in adolescence [PDF file]. In Adelson, J. (Ed.), *Handbook of
adolescent psychology*, pp. 159-187. Retrieved from
https://www.researchgate.net/profile/James_Marcia/publication/233896997_Identity_
in_adolescence/links/0deec52ea6ae66e0f8000000/Identity-in-adolescence.pdf

Martin, K. A. (1996). *Puberty, sexuality and the self: Boys and girls at adolescence.*
Retrieved from
https://books.google.com.mt/books?id=0Ah1iF9y5v0C&printsec=frontcover&dq=pu
berty+and+sexuality&hl=en&sa=X&ved=0ahUKEwil8aL5lc_fAhWRzaQKHdTOCd
4Q6AEIJzAA#v=onepage&q=puberty%20and%20sexuality&f=false

McBride, K. (2010). Puberty. In Cavendish, M. (Ed.), *Sex and society, volume 3*, pp. 695-
699. Retrieved from
https://books.google.com.mt/books?id=csX0f7AVM3gC&pg=PA695&dq=pubertal+c
hanges+in+males+and+females&hl=en&sa=X&ved=0ahUKEwiNmZy69snfAhWFE
ywKHa9zDYoQ6AEISjAG#v=onepage&q=pubertal%20changes%20in%20males%2
0and%20females&f=false

Ministry for health, elderly and community care. (2011). *National sexual health strategy*
[PDF file]. Retrieved from
https://deputyprimeminister.gov.mt/en/CMO/Documents/sexual_health_strategy_engl
ish_version.pdf

Moore, S., Rosenthal, D., & Mitchell, A. (1996). *Youth, AIDS and sexually transmitted
diseases.* Retrieved from

12

https://books.google.com.mt/books?id=Zv2l0FYrn44C&printsec=frontcover&dq=sex
ually+transmitted+disease+in+young+people&hl=en&sa=X&ved=0ahUKEwjS_82c4
=
rfAhVEhywKHYmmAqIQ6AEIJzAA#v=onepage&q=sexually%20transmitted%20di
sease%20in%20young%20people&f=false

Pickhardt, C. E. (2010, April 13). Adolescence and the problems of puberty: puberty the
onset of sexual maturity, creates problems for adolescents. *Psychology Today.*
Retrieved December 30, 2018 from
https://www.psychologytoday.com/us/blog/surviving-your-childs-
adolescence/201004/adolescence-and-the-problems-puberty

Pickhardt, C. E. (2016, September 5). Puberty and preoccupation with personal appearance.
Psychology Today. Retrieved January 2, 2019 from
https://www.psychologytoday.com/us/blog/surviving-your-childs-
adolescence/201609/puberty-and-preoccupation-personal-appearance

Ponzetti, J. J. (2016). Sexuality education: Yesterday, today, and tomorrow. In Ponzetti, J. J.
(Ed.), *Evidence-based approaches to sexuality education: A global perspective*, pp. 1-
14. Retrieved from
https://books.google.com.mt/books?id=uPyPCgAAQBAJ&printsec=frontcover&dq=
what+is+sexuality+education&hl=en&sa=X&ved=0ahUKEwjdvq-
NiOjfAhUGkiwKHV7FDIkQ6AEIJzAA#v=onepage&q=what%20is%20sexuality%2
0education&f=false

Rufus, A. (2009, May 26). Losing virginity? Just "get it over with". Brooke Shields on losing
virginity: get it over with. *Psychology Today.* Retrieved January 12, 2019 from
https://www.psychologytoday.com/us/blog/stuck/200905/losing-virginity-just-get-it-
over

Russell, B. (2018, October 30). Dating, sex, and how to say no: learning how to say no to
what you don't want is a life-changer. Not only will you feel more comfortable and
secure, you will be truly empowered. *The Good men project.* Retrieved January 13,
2019 from https://goodmenproject.com/featured-content/dating-sex-and-how-to-say-
no-bbab/

Schroeder, E. (2009). Introduction. In Schroeder, E., & Kuriansky, J. (Eds.), *Sexuality
education: past, present, and future [4 Volumes]*, pp. xix-xxi. Retrieved from
https://books.google.com.mt/books?id=EZJzCQAAQBAJ&printsec=frontcover&dq=

sexual+education&hl=en&sa=X&ved=0ahUKEwiMg_zkxObfAhXEMewKHcFvCP
UQ6AEILDAB#v=onepage&q=sexual%20education&f=false

Smith, M. T., Moore, S., & Rosenthal, D. (2016). *Sexuality in adolescence: The digital
generation.* Retrieved from
https://books.google.com.mt/books?id=9gZXCgAAQBAJ&printsec=frontcover&dq=
puberty+and+sexuality&hl=en&sa=X&ved=0ahUKEwil8aL5lc_fAhWRzaQKHdTO
Cd4Q6AEIXDAJ#v=onepage&q=puberty%20and%20sexuality&f=false

Symons, D. (1979). *The evolution of human sexuality.* New York, N.Y.: Oxford University
Press, Inc.

Thies, K. M., & Travers, J. F. (2005). *Growth and development through the lifespan.*
Retrieved from
https://books.google.com.mt/books?id=g4YKCgbYs2EC&pg=PA149&dq=challenges
+on+sexual+identity+during+puberty&hl=en&sa=X&ved=0ahUKEwi8l8GulsrfAhW
LiiwKHcp1DTYQ6AEIOjAD#v=onepage&q=challenges%20on%20sexual%20identi
ty%20during%20puberty&f=false

Villanueva, S. (2015, December 8). Teenage stress: addressing the pressures teens face in
today's fast-paced world. Retrieved January 2, 2019 from
https://www.psychologytoday.com/us/blog/how-parent-teen/201512/teenage-stress

Williams, R. C. S. (2016, December 13). Why teens opt not to have sex. *Psychology Today.*
Retrieved on January 12, 2019 from https://www.psychologytoday.com/us/blog/sex-
sexuality-and-romance/201612/why-teens-opt-not-have-sex

Wood, D., Crapnell, T., Lau, L., Bennett, A., Lotstein, D., Ferris, M., & Kuo, A. (2017).
Emerging Adulthood as a critical stage in the life course. In Halfon, N., Forrest.,
Lerner, R., & Faustman, E. (Eds.), *Handbook of life course health development*, pp.
123-143. Retrieved from https://link.springer.com/chapter/10.1007/978-3-319-47143-
3_7#citeas